£9.99

Violin part

the best of grade .

Violin

A compilation of the best Grade 4 violin pieces ever selected by the major examination boards

Selected and edited by Jessica O'Leary

FABER $f\!f$ MUSIC

© 2012 by Faber Music Ltd
This edition first published in 2012
Bloomsbury House
74–77 Great Russell Street
London WC1B 3DA
Music processed by Jackie Leigh
Design by Økvik Design
Cover image: Stockbyte (skd282880sdc)
Printed in England by Caligraving Ltd
All rights reserved

ISBN10: 0-571-53694-8
EAN13: 978-0-571-53694-8

To buy Faber Music publications or to find out about the full range of titles available
please contact your local music retailer or Faber Music sales enquiries:

Faber Music Limited, Burnt Mill, Elizabeth Way, Harlow CM20 2HX
Tel: +44 (0)1279 82 89 82   Fax: +44 (0)1279 82 89 83
sales@fabermusic.com   fabermusicstore.com

Audio tracks 23 and 24 (accompaniment) recorded at Wedgwood Studios, Surrey, 2005
All other audio tracks recorded at Barn Cottage Studio, July 2012
Performed by Jessica O'Leary (violin) and Robin Bigwood (piano)

Engineered by Robin Bigwood
℗ 2012 Faber Music Ltd © 2012 Faber Music Ltd

Contents

The following pieces are included in the Trinity 2010–15 Grade 4 examination syllabus:
Prelude (Cohen): LIST A
Sometime Maybe (Wedgwood): LIST B

The performers

Jessica O'Leary is a professional violinist, teacher, ABRSM examiner and seminar presenter. She has toured and recorded extensively as a member of the Academy of St Martin in the Fields, and has performed with Madonna, Led Zeppelin, the London Symphony Orchestra and the Royal Opera House.

Robin Bigwood is a freelance pianist and harpsichordist, performing with Passacaglia, Feinstein Ensemble, Britten Sinfonia and as a soloist. He also works as a sound engineer and producer.

Track 1: Tuning note A

Rondino

from 'The Young Violinist's Repertoire Book 4'

PERFORMANCE 2
ACCOMPANIMENT 3

The opening of this lively piece is technically easy, so concentrate on the character and the accents. Keep the chords clear by swinging your left arm under the violin more than usual so that the top string rings freely.

Parashkev Hadjiev
arr. de Keyser and Waterman

Con Contento from Concerto in D major

from '3 Concertos for Violin and Orchestra'

PERFORMANCE ④
ACCOMPANIMENT ⑤

Bring sophistication and shape to your performance with elegant lifted up-bows and gentle swells in dynamics. Keep the tempo relaxed and steady throughout.

Georg Philipp Telemann (1681–1767)
arr. Köhs Andreas

Think about gaps.

Rondeau from 'Abdelazer'

from 'Superpieces 2'

You may know this rondeau as the theme from Benjamin Britten's *The Young Person's Guide to the Orchestra*. Stark dynamic contrasts and crisp string crossings will help create a strong performance.

Henry Purcell (1659–1695)
arr. Mary Cohen

Prelude

from 'Technique Takes Off'

Play the melodic line alone first of all and then sneak the chords in, ensuring that you keep the rhythm accurate. It's fun to play this in different acoustics – try every room at home to hear the effect.

Mary Cohen

* Blocked fifth: prepare the chord by placing 1st finger across 2 strings before playing.

Preludio from Sonata in G minor

PERFORMANCE 9
ACCOMPANIMENT 10

This is a stately piece which works well in performance. The shifting is straightforward and the phrase shapes can be exaggerated to create a stylish finish.

Antonio Vivaldi (1678–1741)

Scottish Brawl

from 'The Young Violinist's Early Music Collection'

This energetic piece sounds great with lifted up-bows in bars 2, 6, 13, etc. Keep the music flowing in the gentler middle section and be bold with the dynamic contrasts.

Pierre Attaingnant (*c.*1494–1552)

arr. Edward Huws Jones

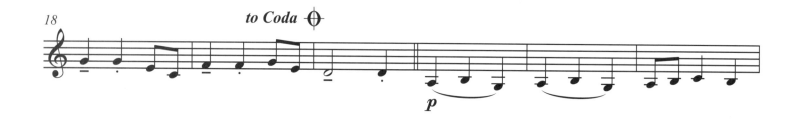

Air Polonais from Sonata in G

Op. 10 No. 2

This is a dramatic movement and precise preparation will be rewarded! There is a lot of interaction with your pianist so make sure you rehearse the ensemble – it will create a fantastically exciting performance.

RONDO

Carl Maria von Weber (1786–1826)

Virelai

Op. 4 No. 3

PERFORMANCE 15
ACCOMPANIMENT 16

If you like melodies, you will love this piece! It flows well and with a little shifting the *legato* quality is easily maintained. Be bold with your sense of expression – can the audience hear every nuance?

Edward Elgar (1857–1934)

La Cinquantaine

PERFORMANCE 17
ACCOMPANIMENT 18

This lovely piece needs to be played with elegance and poise, so beautifully lifted up-bows and careful phrase endings are essential. The harmonics will be more reliable with clean strings and fresh rosin!

Gabriel-Marie (1852–1928)

Mazurka

from 'The Young Violinist's Repertoire Book 3'

PERFORMANCE 19
ACCOMPANIMENT 20

This spirited piece needs a full tone at the start, so try to get your arm-weight into the string
for the bow-strokes. Clear dynamic contrasts will bring the music to life.

Nathalia Baklanova
arr. de Keyser and Waterman

Hindu Song from 'Sadko'

from 'Universal Violin Album'

PERFORMANCE [21]
ACCOMPANIMENT [22]

Bring out the plaintive quality of the melody by moving the bow towards the fingerboard and stretching out the semiquavers a little. Maintain poise at the end until the piano sound completely vanishes – your audience will be mesmerised!

Nikolaj Rimskij-Korsakov (1844–1908)
arr. Peter Kolman

Fly me to the Moon (In Other Words)

from 'Jazz Sessions'

It is a treat to have a jazz trio backing to play along with! Start by playing the rhythms accurately, counting the rests carefully; then relax into the 'swung' rhythms. The section from bar 45 is a written out improvisation so you can adapt it if you like.

Bart Howard

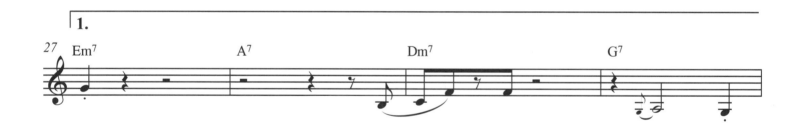

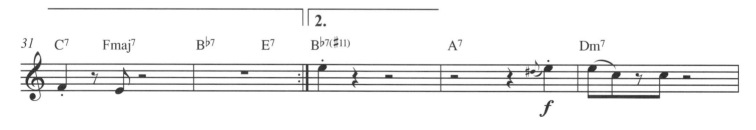

This piece can also be accompanied on the piano using the chords provided above the violin part.

Glass

from 'Unbeaten Tracks'

This lovely contemporary piece needs warm vibrato and clear rhythms. Use lots of *flautando*, where the bow is tilted and floats over the strings by the fingerboard. You can experiment with left-hand fingerings to keep the *legato* quality.

Graham Fitkin

23

Sometime Maybe

from 'Jazzin' About'

This engaging piece needs to flow, so make sure you carefully control your bow speed.
Play with exact rhythms to begin with, but then relax them as the mood takes you!

Pam Wedgwood

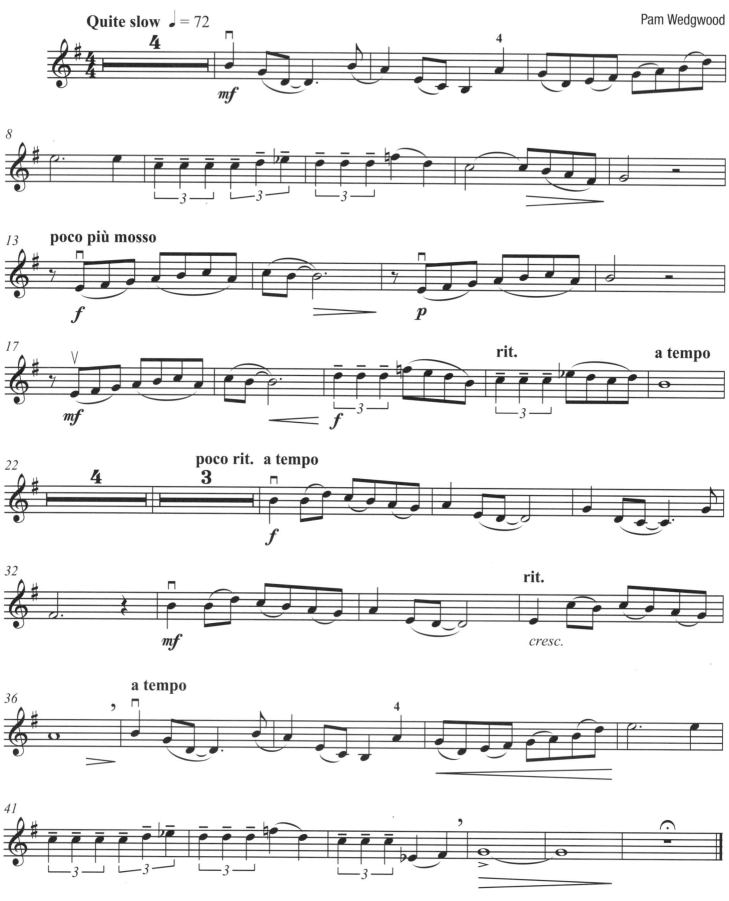